Underfoot

Frank Varela

MARCH/Abrazo Press
Chicago

Acknowledgements

"Electric Cowboys" and "Paulina in the Shadows" appeared originally in *Revista Chicano-Riqueña*, Vol. X, No.3, Summer 1982. Early versions of "Manhattan Circa 1958" and "The End of Time" were published in *The Americas Review*, Vol. 17, No. 1, Spring 1989. "Night Music" was published in *Ariel XI*, Long Grove, Illinois: Triton College, 1993.

Manufactured in the United States of America

Cover art: Benjamin Varela
Photography: Diana Solis
Book design: Cynthia Gallaher

Library of Congress Cataloging-in-Publication Data
Varela, Franklyn P., 1949
Serpent Underfoot poems
include translations
ISBN 1-877-636-11-8
I. Title
II. Puerto Rican Poetry
93-077185
CIP

Dedication

The book for
Ellen and Vincent
who mean so much in my life

My deepest thanks to Carlos Cumpián
for his guidance and support

My thanks to David Garcia, Karen Barrett
and Karen Mensch
for their sharp eyes in the final editing

Serpent Underfoot

Contents

Preface

Energy is eternal.
It exists
in two forms:
you, the reader,
and me, these poems.

Prefacio

La energía es eterna;
existe en dos formas:
usted, el lector,
y yo, en estos poemas.

(Translated by the author)

Manhattan Cerca de 1958

Traductor: Luis Felipe Díaz, Ph.D.

I

En soledad de Carmelitas
mi tía vivía
en una vecindad
de estirados Plymouths
y chevis enmohecidos.
Todos los domingos
mi madre ofrecía
una llamada hermana
a la dama soledad
en cuya casa
espíritus chismeaban
sobre la muerte.
Era el otoño;
desde más allá del Atlántico,
un crudo viento borrascoso
nos urgía hacia el refugio
y a la oscuridad.
La lluvía transformaba
las luces de la calle
en supernovas.
"Vigilen sus pasos ,"
advertía nuestra madre
según cruzabamos
las calles saturadas
por la lluvia.
Otros viajeros impacientes,
por nuestra ruta,
a empujones
nos pasaron
para desvanecerse
en vapores.

Manhattan Circa 1958

I

In Carmelite solitude
my aunt lived
in a neighborhood
of big-finned Plymouths
old-rusted Chevies.
Every Sunday
mama paid a sisterly call
on lady solitude;
in whose flat
spirits gossiped
about the dead.
I remember an autumn day
and a raw bluster
that urged us
forward to shelter
and darkness.
The rain made
the streetlights
go supernova.
"Mind your step,"
admonished mama
as we crossed
rain-dampened streets.
Other travellers
impatient with
our journey
jostled past us
and faded into vapors.

Sigo diciéndome
que tenía ya los nueve años,
casi un hombre,
pero uno sigue detenido
en las garras
de sombras,
murmullos sin personas,
y mi padre con rabia,
nunca llegó:
"No hay seguridad", dijo.
Un hombre murió ejecutado
en el pasillo de la tía.
Leo las noticias,
láminas y textos
colocados en la página doce
junto al comercial
para depilar cabellos.
Un guardia
buscando por todo el mundo,
como Errol Flynn,
en cuclillas
junto al cuerpo
mirando fijamente
el precio del pecado.
Una mano impresa
de sangre
fue todo lo que quedó
para destellar imágenes
de bullicio;
inefable violencia
dicha dentro
de las meticulosas hélices
de los dedos
de un hombre muerto.

I kept telling myself
that I was all of nine
almost a man
but one still held
in the clutches
of shadows
disembodied whispers
my father enraged
who never came:
"It isn't safe,"
he said.
A man died
execution style
in auntie's lobby.
I read the news
pictures and text
tucked away
on page twelve
beside an advertisement
for hair removal.
A copper looking
for all the world
like Errol Flynn
hunkered down
beside the body
grimly staring
at the wages of sin.
A hand print of blood was all
that remained to spark
images of mayhem;
unspeakable violence told
within the meticulous helixes
of a dead man's fingertips.

Podía sentir
el pulso de mi madre
latir,
a través de sus guantes.
"Arriba, arriba,
por las escaleras."
Bajo las luces resplandecientes
retorcidos espectros
salteaban hacia atrás
y hacia el frente.
Cerré mis ojos
y murmuré encantamientos,
pero en el infierno de Dante
voces airadas,
hombre mujer,
ángeles incandescentes,
profirieron injurias
contra el mundo,
contra sus vidas,
unos contra los otros.
¿Y corrimos—
mi madre y yo—
como fugitivos desesperados,
por una película de espanto,
de segunda?
Era domingo—
el día del Señor—
que para algo
tendría que contar.

II

Odié dormir
junto a ella
luchando por la sábana,

I could feel
mama's pulse beat
through the leather
of her glove.
"Up, up, upstairs."
Under glaring lights
contorted shadows
vaulted back and forth.
I closed my eyes
and mumbled incantations
but in Dante's hell
angry voices
man woman
incandescent angels
spat invectives
against the world
their lives
each other.
Did we run
like desperate fugitives
in a second-rate thriller?
It was Sunday—
the Lord's day—
that had to count
for something.

II

We'd spend the night—
our Sunday routine
mama on the sofa
me in bed with auntie.
I hated sleeping
with the woman
fighting for blanket

escuchando su ronquido
asincopado
con el tic tac del reloj.
El me mantuvo despierto
como lo hicieron
los fantasmas,
espíritus por todas partes
alborotando las tablas del piso,
volátiles cortinas
que murmuran
para negar el sueño.
Pero más que nada
me espanté con visiones
de muertos familiares,
mirando fijamente
sus retratos
en el vestíbulo.
Estaba asustado,
pero la visita
a la oscuridad
pagó sus dividendos
a un niño ansioso
enamorado de sus regalos.
Una vez más
mi tía me dio
una gorrita
de guerra civil
en gris rebelde.
Y entre sorbos
de Bustelo me entregó
una bolsa arrugada.
Busqué en el saco
para encontrar
el tesoro oculto.
Sonrió y pude captar
el destello de oro
se sus dientes frontales.

hearing her snore
syncopate with
the ticking clock.
It kept me up
as did ghosts
spirits everywhere
troubling floorboards
swaying curtains
and murmuring
to deny dreams
but most of all
I dreaded visions
of the family dead
leering out
from their pictures
in the foyer.
I was scared
but the visit
into darkness
paid dividends
for a greedy boy
in love with presents.
Auntie once gave me
a Civil War kepi
in rebel grey.
Between sips
of "Bustelo"
she handed me
a wrinkled Macy's bag.
I gutted the sack
to reveal treasure inside.
She smiled
and I caught the glint
of gold around
her front tooth.

Nunca pensé
que fuera atractiva
hasta más tarde.
Estaba en el álbum familiar,
una joven mujer
posando en las acera
durante del verano
de Coney Island.
Debió haber sido
un día ventoso.
Aparece aguantando
su elegante sombrero
como una modelo
brazo con brazo—
¡y oigan esto!—
con papá.
Removí el retrato
del plástico
que lo cubría
y al voltearlo leí
"Querido",
y luego: "Marta".

III

Debo haber luchado,
al igual que en Gettysburg,
cien veces
con alaridos rebeldes,
metrallas
sonidos de mortero.
Rígidos estaban
los nervios de mi tía.
Podía leer tensión,
miradas nerviosas
tiradas hacia mi senda,
ojos que telegrafiaban

I never thought
her attractive
until much later.
She was in the family album
a young woman
posing on boardwalk
Coney Island summer.
It must have been
a windy day
because she's
holding down
her fancy hat
like a model
arm in arm with—
get this—papa.
I removed the picture
from its sleeve
turned it over
and read:
Querido and then Marta.

III

I must have
fought Gettysburg
a hundred times
with rebel yells
grapeshot
mortar sounds.
Auntie's nerves
went raw.
I could read tension
nervous glances
thrown my way
eyes telegraphing

el regaño
de solterona.
Una advertencias,
dos advertencias:
"muchacho salvaje,
muchacho malo",
vociferó.
Y lloré con
un "ay" de dolor,
pero no con mi voz.
(No era mi voz).
Era la de ella.

IV

Y no era ya un niño
sino un hombre
parado al lado
de su cama,
contemplando
mientras ella se fugaba
en un profundo silencio.
Una enfermera llegó:
"Ya es hora".
Y yo soy Lázaro
con huesos crujientes
y lamentos sin quebrar,
susurrando.
Señora soledad:
¿Te amé alguna vez
o soñé tus penas?
¿Y en ese día de lágrimas
era yo un hombre
o era un niño perdido
en el espiral
de una tarde de Domingo?

a spinster's rebuke.
One warning
two warnings:
"Wild boy, bad boy,"
she snapped.
I cried out
with an "Ow" of pain
but not with my voice
(That wasn't my voice)
it was hers.

IV

I was no longer
a child
but a grown up
standing
by her bedside
watching her slip
into a deeper silence.
A nurse walked in:
"It's time."
I am Lazarus
with creaking bones
and unmended sorrows
whispering:
Lady solitude
did I ever love you
or did I dream your sorrows
and on that day of tears
was I a man or still a boy
lost in the spiral
of a Sunday afternoon?

Esa mañana
ella ofreció
sus agobios
como la única posesión:
come y prueba
su amargura.
Y lloré
con un "ay" de dolor,
pero no con su voz,
(Esa no era su voz)
era la mía.
Absoluto pasado,
absoluto futuro
que convergen
en un inevitable ahora.
Un cornetín de ejército,
distante,
me pide la retirada.
Y soy un niño una vez más
en Manhattan, cerca de 1958.

That morning
she gave up
her burden like
an only possession:
eat and taste
its bitterness.
I cried out
with an "Ow" of pain
but not with her voice
(That wasn't her voice)
it was mine.
Absolute past
absolute future
converge into
the unavoidable now.
A distant bugle
sounds retreat.
I'm a boy once more
in Manhattan circa 1958.

Electric Cowboys

O when I was six
hissing tubes
and light chinks
gave me life
as I moved closer
to the mother warmth
of my Zenith Royal.
I was a child
held in the ecstasy
of time and technology
to behold electric cowboys
every afternoon
so when the Hop or Gene
even the singing duo
Dale and Roy
rode on palomino splendor
I knew
I honestly knew
I was in heaven.

O I would sit
seventeen stories
above Brooklyn concrete.
My small arms reached
for celluloid dreams
of electric cowboys
singing under
a whiskey sky
and when mama came home
I went for my gun
and shot her dead.
Death was a game played
in the desert valleys
of the synchronized west.

O my heart quaked
whenever my cowboys
met their deaths
but in their songs
ran notes I never heard
and the western song
became a dirge
with every Indian
and Mexican spent;
while I sat beguiled
in the shadows
of the flickering images
and when they rode
on the screen
I thought
I honestly thought
I was in heaven.

The End of Time

The early evening news...

6:05 P.M.
Liverpool's vaporized;
New York's dust.
The great powers
are at war—WW III.
In Chicago
the desperate claw
their way from ground zero
or leap from
high-towered aeries
into the canyons
of the Loop.

6:10 P.M.
our President
announces:
"As Commander-in-Chief
I have ordered
the military
to launch an attack
upon the Soviet Union
and her allies."

Boom goes Moscow
boom Kiev
boom Hanoi.

But here in Bucktown
boys shoot hoops
in Holstein Park.
Latino lovers stroll
arm in arm

a final memory.
The common noise
of a softball game
dopplerizes something
by Ruben Blades:
loud-louder-loudest-
loudest-louder-loud.

Death will come
to Bucktown
but he will find
a community of families—
listing from
Alvarez to Zayas—
a people sobered
by the melancholy
of the Conquest
the Inquisition
the thousand revolutions
that stoked fires
beneath stoic hearts—
this their final dignity:
families sitting
on the stoops
of their two flats
waiting for the Rapture.

6:15 P.M.
a 20 megaton device
    implodes
        explodes.
    Matter compresses
        then dissolves.
    Overhead
      a new day
          an evil sun is born.

The Raccoons
of Humboldt Park

How out of place
you seem
ambling down
North Avenue.

Are you lost
or out to explore
dreaded city
by the lake?

There's more found
than lost in you.
That bandit's face
harbors sly
impenetrable
eclipsing moon.

Your rings remind me
of Cheshire Cat
one instant there
next gone.

My wife's worry: dogs—
mangy creatures.
The strays'll get
out of your way
than risk
tooth and claw.

But I never thought
raccoons favored
Humboldt Park.

Yes Humboldt Park
ten city blocks
set down on prairie
open to the sky.

On Sundays
lovers wander
serpentine paths
when summer leaves
or autumnal splendor
dress the trees
in colors.

Only public buildings
betray the presence
of another power—
graffiti's blasphemy.

Let's consider
if raccoons favor
Humboldt Park
why not other fauna?

Imagine bison
thundering across
the flatlands
as in the days
before DuSable
LaSalle and Father Marquette.

Or spy
stalking antelope
a golden shadow
lost among the whites
of Queen Anne's Lace.

Wouldn't it be marvelous
if in the lagoon
near the boathouse
the one done in prairie school
beavers craved outlets
for stagnant waters
birthing mighty Humboldt River?

In one generation
time curves
in on itself
and the park spills
beyond its borders.

Whitetails
alertskittish
headsupdown
nibble
tender shoots
while rusting cars
become ferny
forlorned relics
of another era
and men women
regain paradise
no more curse
of sin's taint.

Funny how
raccoons can
change a city.

Von Humboldt
himself would
never believe—
ivy scaling up Sears Tower;

bachelor buttons
carpeting the Kennedy
from Jefferson Park
to Stony Island;
fauna and flora
repossessing
the kingdom of man
at the twilight
of creation.

And while
buses cars
no longer
rumble up
Michigan Avenue
manikins
stare dumbly
at a sky
never seen
so blue.

Tierra Negra

Traductor: Luis Felipe Díaz, Ph.D.

I

Abro surcos
en mi jardín,
con cuidado,
para no perturbar
las raíces.
Rica es la tierra,
por las lluvias
de pasadas estaciones.
En mis mejores días
puedo hurgar
en el suelo
y unir mi alma
al mundo verde:
tarracota y escarole
bálsamo de limón y salvia.
¡Envidia el poder
de la tierra negra
antes que
el barro enrojecido
se asome
a las vista
y las piedras
maldigan al granjero!

II

Hace años
abuelo habías dispuesto
diez acres
de Cibuco

Black Earth

"Time, like an ever rolling stream,
bears all its sons away."
(Our God, Our Help in Ages Past)

I

I hoe furrows
in my garden
careful not
the roots
to disturb.
The land
is rich
with decay
and past seasons.
On my best days
I can reach
into the soil
and marry my soul
with the green world—
tarragon and escarole
lemon balm and sage
envy the power
of black earth
before bloody clay
seeps into view
and no stones
the farmer's curse.

II

Years ago
grandfather cleared
ten acres
by *Cibuco*

para arrancarle
el trabajo
al rojo barro.
Los retratos familiares
revelaron al lánguido hombre
de amplios hombros
y de silueta gris
contra el azul cielo;
con polvo manchando
su camisa anaranjada
en los rudos días
sin misericordia.
Aún así amaba la tierra
y plantó ese amor
entre sus hijos,
aún cuando el viento
los dispersó
por lugares distantes.
Llorando el Jueves Negro
abuelo observaba
desde el balcón
de la casa rosa
una carreta
cargar a su gente
en su viaje al norte
de Babilonia,
y al exilio.

III

Años más tarde
vi la casa
de la finca inmersa
en la maleza crecida;
a la larga se desplomó
el granero;

to wrench subsistence
from red clay.
Family pictures
revealed a lanky
broad-shouldered man
silhouetted gray
against an aqua sky
red dust staining
his shirt orange
in days rough
without mercy.
He loved his land
and seeded that love
among his children
even when the wind
scattered them
to a distant place.
Grieving Black Thursday
grandfather watched
from the verandah
of the pink house
as an ox-cart
carried his people
for their journey
north to Babylon
and exile.

III

Years later
I saw
the farmhouse set
among overgrown fields,
the barn long collapsed;

sólo las vigas
del marco del norte
se mantuvieron firmes
contra el cielo tuquesa.
Yo arranqué
los bejucos del pasto
y desmigajé barro
entre mis dedos;
por esto los hombres
viven y mueren.

IV

Tu alma me habló
esa noche cuando
el viento perturbó
el tul que rodeaba mi cama.
Estuve acostado
medio observando
una mariposa nocturna
golpearse sin sentido
contra la luz.
El mueblario del cuarto
me recordaba de otro tiempo
cuando los hombres
definían sus vidas
por el trabajo
de sus manos.
Las pisadas hacían
que las tablas
del piso crujieran.
Sentí tu presencia
en el pasillo.

only the ribs
of the north framing
stood raised against
the turquoise sky.
I uprooted cane grass
and crumbled clay
between my fingers;
this is what men
live and die for.

IV

Your soul spoke
to me that night
when the wind
troubled the netting
around my bed.
I laid half watching
a moth batter
itself senseless
against the light.
The room's furniture
reminded me
of another age
when men defined their lives
through the labor
of their hands.
Footsteps sent
the floorboards creaking.
I felt your presence
in the hallway.

Y al abrirse la puerta,
allí estabas:
un espectro mudo,
vestido de blanco,
hechizado por un extraño
como yo
en búsqueda
de su pasado.

V

Abuelo,
he viajado desde lejos
a este lugar de silencio
donde tus afanes
te quebraron antes
de tu descanso.
Mi pueblo
tomó tus huesos
y los depositó
en la negra tierra.
Mas duerme en paz, abuelo,
pues nada destruye el amor.

The door opened
and there you stood:
a mute specter
dressed in white
haunted by a stranger
in search of his past.

V

Abuelo I have travelled far
to this place of silence
where your labors drained you
before your final rest.
My people took your bones
and set them down into black earth.
Sleep easy grandfather
nothing kills love.

Street Songs

I.
The Seven-African Gods

Crazy Willie waited
near the entrance of Humboldt Park,
motioned for me to hurry.
He ignored my outstretched hand
and fell into step beside me.

"It all started with the Seven-African Gods.
You see, bro, we stopped worshipping
the Seven-African Gods."

I was perplexed.
"You're not making any sense."

Crazy Willie winked,
hummed *música de Machito.*
I noticed that as we walked
deeper into *el parque,*
reality shifted:
oaks lengthened into *palmas;*
elms—strangler figs;
the grey sky of winter—turquoise.

"*Tú sabes,*" Crazy Willie said
looking over his shoulder,
"*cuando* we stopped worshipping
the Seven-African *Dioses*, they turned on us."

Numbed, it dawned on me.
"They got even?"

"*Claro*, damn right, spics were banished to Chicago."

II.
In a Bar on Division Street

Crazy Willie's a genius,
smarter than Einstein,
scarier than Alien.
"You know, bro,
I could make a million."

I turned to take in his wisdom.

"*Hombre*, I ain't shittin' you," he said,
while tapping his head. "It's all here."

Crazy Willie swirled the last of his bottle
and drank it down cold.
He called out to the barkeep,
stuck two fingers out,
and pointed to the empties.

"I have it all in my head.
It's a story about the nastiest thing in *el mundo*."

"So tell." I felt his hand tighten
around my arm.

"It's a book about a gangbanger
who lives long enough to be a *viejo*.
Only he ain't got no peace."

"Why's that?"

"He's haunted by every guy he iced.
Shit, the dude forgot that nothing ever dies."

The Gardener

I.
Grace Note

I shake off
grey reluctance
to inspect
my garden.
The snow
collapses
beneath
the weight
of my boot
and the air
makes my
eyes water.
I can
still gather
oregano
or thyme
(fresh and green)
in the middle
of January.
Push aside
the snow
it's there—
small miracles
defying winter.

II.
Land

I dream land so rich
that if I were to walk on it
I would be transformed—
bones into tubers;
my hair
silk of corn.

III.
Sorrel

Sorrel's tang
reminds me
of ecstacy—
bitterness
mixed with candy.
My son
loves sorrel.
His coffee bean eyes
gleam mischief
hooked on bitter herbs.
Perhaps he'll become
a cunning man
versed in earth law
and herbal science:
pick mistletoe
when moon
is six days old;
burn myrrh
to purify;
and lavender
sweet elf leaf
ah...that one's for love.

IV.
Music

Death is but a hush—
an extended chord of silence,
the earth fills with music.

Country Club Satori

Walking through the Colorado Country Club
toward the granite face of the Cheyenne Mountains
and listening to the voice of God
whispering to me from across the 15th green—

St. Paul would've been astounded.

One Hundred Million Years Ago

One hundred million years ago an asteroid
as flat as an Illinois cornfield
certainly larger than a LaSalle Street ego
crashed into the Mesozoic world
of pterodactyls and iguanodons.
Imagine the roar of an intergalactic
object hurled 40,000 m.p.h. through a sky
bluer than a chunk of turquoise
a comet's tail a 1,000 miles long
super heating the atmosphere
to temperatures unknown
since the dawn of creation.
Nesting duckbill maiasaurs
must have peered up, green eyes
uncomprehending a sight no earthly beastie
knew or ever predicted.
What thought or sensation surged
through reptilian minds?
And when they died
did a maiasaur brood her clutch
in the shelter of her love?
Love you say, you say love?
Love as between consenting partners
in the age of television?
Or was it something beyond
the whispers of carnal affection?
Was it life affirming life
even to the threshold of death?
One hundred million years ago
love was love
even in the age of dinosaurs.

Paulina in the Shadows

Shadows hook like claws
and you're hung by your heels
like some Halloween effigy
to scare off the dead.
Last night Paulina
made crazy by love
slit her wrists
thinking of Seneca and Him
sat gazing at a distant star
while a thin red angry comet
blazed across the tub's white porcelain.

Madonna

Bayamon, Puerto Rico

I

In cutoffs and sneakers
Botticelli angels
tender off-key Christmas carols
to the passengers
of Bus No. 9,
but no one obliges
discordant praises
for Christ the King.
The little bus—
blue enamel dented—
wallows westbound
down the Kennedy
where palm trees
stand military straight
casting shadows
on verdant tropicals.
The rush-hour throng
crams the aisle
shoulder to shoulder
hip against hip
unintentional intimacy
eliciting neither
blush nor pardon.
The bus stops;
an old woman dressed
in a sleeveless gown
her face a mass of wrinkles
that would drive
a cartographer batty
eyes the congestion
and motions the bus on.

II

Bus No. 9 passes
cinder block homes
through *Bayamon's* narrows
where hawkers sell
oranges and limes
plantain chips
and sugar cane.
Seated in back
a Black Madonna
adorned in red
with shopping
at her feet—
and she's beautiful
with copper hair
and caramel skin.
Angels repeat off-key carols
to each boarding passenger;
then with out-stretched hands
collect their urchin's mite.
La Madona never forgets
those who remember
holy days and Palestine.
They've collected
not even a dollar
for their songs.

III

Angered *La Madona*
promises she'll crush
the serpent underfoot
but today gives
her bus angels
a crisp twenty.
Who is this generous woman
with angry eyes?

La Madona picks
up her parcels
and walks up the aisle.
As she passes
a young pharisee,
he nudges his friend
and makes the sign
for madness.

The Shark

St. John, U.S. Virgin Islands

I

A pink rain descends.
Flame trees are
weeping petals upon
a dream landscape:
strangler figs
and monkey-no-climbs
umbrella trees and
buttonwoods. This
land absorbs you,
strips you clean.
Bones are for new
purposes, skull for
hermit crab, hair in
hummingbird's nest.
And I am a stranger
in this land, working
for Mr. Clark, southern
gentleman, a purveyor
of pleasure for old
Yankees seeking bliss.

II

The road sends its quiver
through the flesh
of my neighbor's thighs.
Allison—my employer's
daughter—nurses me

from yesterday's encounter
with sea urchins.
The toes on my right foot
are swollen sausage fat,
and I'm useless.
Mr. Clark plans a walk
with a tour group across
the narrows of Leinster
Bay, where the apples
of the manchineel trees
are lethal with toxins.
I bump along as extra
baggage watching Allison
watching me. Green eyes
stare back unafraid
with bemused detachment.
A certain tension exists
between us. Mr. Clark,
good Baptist, would
never approve, but
at night in her bed,
we have angry sex.

III

Death is never far
from the sea. Men
died eating apples
at Leinster Bay.
Somewhere near shallows,
the shark becomes
a ripple under
skins of water.
I cannot say when
I became the shark,

but watching it from
shore, I understood
a deeper lust.
Perhaps it was
a conjunction of stars
or the liquid voice
of the sea which
transformed me.
Knowing, yet unknowing,
which me was me?
Gliding with an ease
I cannot comprehend,
wisdom—terrible and
pure—should never be
gained. Wasn't that
the lesson of Adam
and Eve? "Call them
back." Did I scream
that or did I fall
into the abyss
of her green eyes?

IV

Funny how people react
to danger. Motion slows
as if liberated from
the laws of physics.
On shore, I pushed away
liver-spotted hands,
ignored aged faces
to witness my better self
turn and seek the lower
depths. Later I couldn't
sneak into Allison's bedroom.

I sat on the edge of my bed
watching smoke curl around
the end of my cigarette.
Down the road the neon
of Harry's Calypso Bar
flashed red, flashed off.
A steel drum resonated,
"Belinda's gone to marry."
While on the dance floor,
couples merged, unmerged;
arms waved like sea fans;
and voices eeled
over rock and crevice,
sunless voids where
mermaids once lured men
to death and ecstasy.
That night dreaming dreams,
I did dream of sharks.

My First Wife

Things left unsaid;
a marriage neglected
stillborn
silence
eviscerating
love
an empty rosewood box
on the spindle-legged table
beside our bed.
I hated you
despised myself more.

I remember
a childhood dimmed
to adumbration
a forgotten boredom
pierced suddenly
by words
between my parents.

They were
harsh words
steel-tipped lethal
hurled
without
the polite syncopation
of our lace-curtained world
that fluttered
in a room
where we stood frozen
for all eternity.

Meditation

for Ellen

Over Lake Michigan
    lightning moves
    like the fingers
    of a pianist
    nuancing Chopin.
I've come to witness secrets
    lessons of light and darkness
    brujo magic
    in the sky's thunder.
Remember the film *Black Orpheus*?
Death is a Macumba priest
    dressed as death
    for Carnival.
Tonight I'm Orpheus
    singing old *boleros*
    to my love Euridyce
    who's back
    from lands
    where sleep
    never ends.
And she is...air;
    sacred smoke
    contained beside
    me as woman
    whose impeccable aura
    flashes luminous
    through the pores
    of her skin
    whose texture
    my fingers memorize.

Autobiography

It was never who or what I was.
I am simply who I am
and what I am never depended
on what people thought of me.
That wisdom got drilled into my head
by an iron-willed grandmother
who could out think any man
in the five boroughs of New York.
Identity was never a question
of geography and language
or time and distance. I was
a spic in the United States;
a *gringo* in the land of my
parent's birth. I got it coming
and going, but I never came to sorrow
for skin I never was. I was always
on the outside looking in so call
yourself what you will because
I am who I am and not the who
you think I ought to be.
All I wanted was the impossible:
to be the who I am in a land
unafraid of the me I have become.

Jorge Luis Borges

Labyrinths
lead
to
Minotaur
who
sits
center
waiting
not
with
death
but
riddles.

Eduardo Galeano

History
is
a
plumed
serpent;
its
mouth
drips
ink.

After the Burial

In her bedroom
St. Anthony gazed
disconsolated
from his perch
on the bureau
where mama prayed.
A handkerchief
of Spanish lace
covered auburn;
her fingers measured
bead by bead
the amber-stone rosary
now coiled on her dresser
like a slumbering snake
awaiting
the resurrection
of spring.

Korea: Sympathetic Pain

In soldier dress
uncle appeared
unannounced
like Santa
one Christmas
during the war;
his smooth
unlined face
a tanned moon
lips compressing
a wound's pain
arms clasping papa
who surprised
pirouetted
from his embrace
as if he had
taken shrapnel.

The Scarecrow Boy

This is a love poem; only thing is
there's no difference between pain and love.
I'm the Scarecrow Boy; the kid you hung
by the neck that fall in '58. Christ
in his private hell that was a poor year for love.
Watch the Scarecrow Boy dance: legs flailing,
fingers tearing the strap around his neck.
I'm the Hanged Man; who dealt me these cards?

This is a love poem told in pictures.
Not movies in the theater pictures, but the snaps
in the family album. Here's one, take a look.
Papa has me on his lap. Ain't he the prize though?
All duded up in Sunday best, leaning back on his chair
as if he owned the world. Mama's in satin, the perfect
'50s form-fitting sequins and pearls Latina.
She's smiling—thank God someone's happy here.

This is a love poem in the city of death,
where ghosts chase shadows in the pale moonlight.
The Scarecrow Boy wants possession of my soul.
At first I resisted his blandishments,
but there's no way of keeping him out—
locks, bars, even a blanket over my head,
useless. He comes whenever I'm deep in sleep
and spirits into my body like a special effect.
Remember *Invasion of the Body Snatchers*?
One night I turn in and return different.
The eyes that stare back aren't mine.
I'm him again, the Scarecrow Boy.

This is a love poem for members only.
Membership is free, the only requirement:
become a Scarecrow Boy just like me.
Transformation is almost painless—
it hurts only when you love.

Night Music

Under a lamppost singing
five hungry souls evoke
shadows with their harmonies.

Under a lamppost chanting
five alchemists
transmute a leadened
Brooklyn night
into dreams
of golden stardom.

A police siren
distant, urgent
syncopates their music
into cool jazz.

Five hungry souls
under a lamppost singing
shatter the anarchy
of a darkened Brooklyn street
and become immortal.

Music is order
order soul.
Aristotle would've
loved doo-wop.

Building a House

I

Windows

The art of windows
isn't about shutting
something out;
it is,
in the final analysis,
the art of holding
something back.

II

Doors

What purpose did God have
in creating doors?
Think for a moment
the sublime jest
when the door we think
protects locks us out instead.

III

Doors #2

Closing doors resonate
in consequences unseen.
I've been closing doors
for most of my years.
On the other side
footsteps fall away like
the aspirations of a man
entering mid-life.

In his workshop
carpenter planes
the oak of my doors
measures length and width
careful in detail
because in time wood warps
and so does character.

Something in me hates doors.

IV

Cupboards

There's something
almost human
about cupboards:
observe
neat facades
hiding untidiness
within.

The Sun People

For the sun people
the liquid action of bodies swaying,
the rhythm of Caribbean dance,
whose distillessence
(la salsa Puertorriqueña)
sparks fire—
fiebre humana.

Extraterrestrials

Eminent Lewis Thomas
once wrote
re: contact
w/extraterrestrials:
"I would just
send Bach
but that would
be bragging."
In my letter
dear Lewis,
I'd send them
Willie Colón
and get them dancing.

Walking through the Loop, December 1992

Another day unemployed walking through
the Loop to kill time while waiting
for an interview where I will die
in stages before an interviewer
who's shaking her head as if I'm telling
her an original idea but she's really
in an altered state because she's been
told the same story before and all she
wants to do is go home and finish packing
and board a jet to spend the next five
days in sunny *Cozumel* sipping *margaritas*
while watching locals do interesting
Third World things; but no, instead,
I'm wasting her time; you see between
nine to five this is her job and I would
kill to have it if only she'd oblige me
by nodding off while I invoke the fury
of the Seven-African Gods to drive her
mad with visions of giant *margaritas*
and the very gates of hell.

On the Beach

I'm obsessed about nuclear war.

> You see I'm standing on the beach
> (nod to Nevil Shute's great novel),
> looking at the ocean.

Why ocean?

> I haven't a clue.
> (Honestly it's just a dream,
> nothing really important.)

But have you ever noticed

> that you're never
> really in the ocean
> being devoured,
> let's say, by sharks?

No, it's always

> standing on the beach
> near the ocean.
> Does the symbolism deal
> with mother-longing
> or fear of death?

I'm standing on the beach

> but I'm unsure
> if I'm looking
> at an ocean
> or a big lake.

You see I'm an adopted Chicagoan

      so a lake looks
      as big as an ocean,
      for all I know
      I could be
      on Oak Street beach.

I'm dressed

      (for those who care)
      in a double-breasted number
      by a famous designer.
      I have exquisite dreams.

Suddenly (as dreams go)

      I'm aware of echoes
      in the canyons of the Gold Coast.
      I'm assuming we're in Chicago.

I turn the condominiums

      behind me are abandoned.
      (The super rich are like rats.
      They're the first
      to go when the ship sinks.
      One day they'll even escape death,
      but not today
      this is the day of reckoning.)

The ocean—no lake—is calm.

      Lakes are better than oceans;
      you never get woofed down
      by sharks in a lake;
      unless you live near *Titicaca*

where for generations
    fresh water man-eaters
    have feasted upon the descendants
    of the Great *Inca*.

I'm no longer

    on the beach
    (That's the way of dreams).
    Instead I'm the pilot
    of a multi-billion dollar weapons system.
    The cockpit molds my body
    like mother's womb.

Mach 1, Mach 2...blip, blip

    radar tracks hostiles
    over a horizon
    the pious believed
    fell into the abyss.

Eighty thousand feet

    higher than brave
    Daedalus ever flew,
    time and distance compress.
    Earth yields its vulnerability
    under the digital eye
    of a lasermetric bombsight.

Below filaments of light

    stretch outward
    in lustrous flares.

Creatures—cautious ones—

> step green red red green.
> Who lives in this city
> of quadrants
> parallel roads?

I'm now Gregory Peck;

> and Ava Gardner—
> my sloe-eyed beauty
> from Babylon—
> she's in my arms;
> dare I say it?
> I'm in love.

But love

> doesn't concern us here;
> as a species it never did.

No, the real matter before us is creation—

> first instance
> (spacial/temporal),
> when God in Old Testament splendor
> cleaved darkness from light,
> tree of knowledge,
> tree of life,
> perfection,
> absolute
> incontrovertible
> perfection,
> the only rub,
> free will.

Free will that's what got us into this mess.

> Think about it.
> What's the good
> of free will
> without omnipotence?
> To be god-like
> but without power?

Ladies and gentlemen

> I put it to you this way:
> if we couldn't be gods—
> that's right;
> you're hearing me right—
> if we couldn't be gods
> we should've been ants.

Bitter Coffee

The red hills of *Cibuco*
are spread out along
a horizon of serpents.
The ghosts of my ancestors
return at day's end
to witness the present
as I ponder the past.
I hear their voices
just outside my window
in the rustle of dry leaves
the flutter of wings.
Wasn't it Columbus
who called *Boricua* paradise
the new Eden
of flame trees and mahogany?
Oubao Moin
island of blood
has sorrows
as sharp as bitter coffee.
The history
of my people began
where all journeys begin
with one step forward
and pain
a single bead of sweat.

Author:
My publisher asked me to write a "bio," a traditional third person narrative about my life and art. So I started out by writing, "Franklyn P. Varela is a poet of great clarity and conviction."

But as for clarity, I can't see worth a damn. Nothing is ever clear to me, because I'm nearly blind. If my glasses got any stronger, I'd see Mars on a cloudy day. As for conviction, I'm convinced that a '66 Pontiac GTO was the greatest car ever built—no matter what the Japanese make.

The real story is that I write from the heart. I'm originally from Brooklyn which is a lot like the south side of Chicago—rough and tumbled places endowed with gritty cosmic energy. My work has appeared in *Revista Chicano-Riqueña, The Americas Review*, and *Arte Publico Press*. "The Silver Bay," a children's story, is circulating somewhere on this planet as part of an elementary school reader put out by the Riverside Press.

It took me three years, and a lifetime of courage, to write *Serpent Underfoot*. The title comes by way of my editor, a brilliant guy who's also a fine poet. Read, enjoy, and peace be with you and all the generations hereafter.

Translator:

Luis Felipe Díaz was born in Aguas Buenas, Puerto Rico, and moved with his family to Chicago when he was sixteen. He studied at the University of Puerto Rico and there attained a B.A. in comparative literature. Upon returning to Chicago, he enrolled at the University of Illinois-Chicago where he earned his M.A. His doctoral studies were completed at the University of Minnesota in 1983.

He currently teaches graduate seminars in Spanish literature, Puerto Rican literature and semiotics at the University of Puerto Rico. He has taught at the University of Minnesota, Inter-American University of Puerto Rico, and other institutions of higher learning. A distinguished scholar, he is the author of *Ironía e ideología en La Regenta de Leopoldo Alas*, a critical examination of the use of irony in modern Spanish literature. He is currently working on a book of literary criticism on Puerto Rican literature, which is scheduled for release in 1994. Other scholarly efforts include critical articles and essays on Federico García Lorca, Antonio S. Pedreira, Luis Palos Matos and José de Diego.

Artist:

Benjamin Varela is the author's younger brother, who was also born in Brooklyn. He is also a former amateur wrestler, who represented Puerto Rico in the 1975 Pan American Games and the 1976 Olympics.

He is a graduate of the Madison Area Technical College where he attained an associate's degree in graphic arts. His art has been seen in Chicago area galleries. He is active in the Taller Mexicano de Grabado in the Pilsen community of Chicago.

For additional copies, order from:

MARCH/Abrazo Press
P.O. 2890
Chicago, Illinois 60690
(312)539-9638

Also available to
the book trade from:

Literati & Co.
(708)432-0346